The Promise of

Jacob Biswell

www.jacobbiswell.com

Cover Design: Jacob Biswell

DEDICATION

To Joanna Coe- Herndon & your dad Jack Coe, Sr.
Two champions of Revival in this modern age! Thank you
for paying the price!

To my Children and my Children's Children –
Don't stop seeking, praying, knocking and asking God for
revival!

CONTENTS

ACKNOWLEDGMENTS

To my wife Anna who allowed me to spend many nights up late to write what the Lord was speaking to me.

To the generals of Revival – your stories have caused me to hunger for a move of God in my generation!

i

Foreword

When I hear the word "Revival" the little girl inside of me leaps with excitement. As I read "The Promise of Revival" that same leaping happened again. Psalms 85:6 reads, "Wilt thou not revive us, so they people may rejoice in thee?" We need fresh fire and fresh bread for this day and hour!

I grew up the daughter of a revival carrier. My dad Jack Coe, Sr. was a healing revivalist in the 40's and 50's here in America. I was ruined for revival -that's all I knew. My dad asked the Lord one time, "Am I in the last day revival?" The Lord responded, "Jack, when you were a little boy, what did you see in the stars?" "Lord, first I would look for the little dipper and then I would look for the big dipper!" The Lord responded, "Jack, you are in the little dipper..."

I believe the BIG dipper is coming, and I want to be part of it! Books like this one stir me towards that revival. We need an army of hungry people to rise and join in a burning desire for God to move on us again. "Re" means to do it again - the Promise of Revival is real.

It is time to recoup our spiritual losses and be the Glorious Church without spot or wrinkle (Eph. 5:27). It's time for the people of God to be stirred up towards the Heart of God - that's where Revival begins. Revival is God manifesting His presence in supernatural greatness. Revival makes us aware of our sin and reveals our need for complete dependence on Him.

Let there be a cry in your heart, be stirred, and allow the Holy Spirit to touch you again. Allow your thoughts to be rearranged to match his - grab hold of "The Promise of Revival!" When a fire starts on the inside of you - you'll never be the same!

With Revival Fire,

Joanna Coe-Herndon
Revival Harvest Ministries
Daughter of the late Jack Coe, Sr.

Introduction

I burn for revival. There is nothing I want more than to see a multi-generational, multi-racial, multi-denominational move of God in this hour. This book is birthed out of that desire. My greatest prayer is that you would find yourself stirred, impassioned and empowered to live a lifestyle of Revival – He promises it!

"It shall come about after this That I shall pour out My Spirit on all mankind; And your sons and your daughters will prophesy, Your old men will dream dreams, Your young men will see visions." Joel 2:28 (AMP)

Are you ready for Revival? I thought I was – and then I missed it. I share my journey of chasing after the Holy-Ghost and the times that I almost caught him. Read and be challenged to receive the Promise of Revival!

Jacob Biswell

-Chapter One-

The Promise of Revival

In Acts 2 we read about what could be called the first Christian Revival, on the Day of Pentecost after Peter had preached to the assembled crowd, 3,000 put their trust in Christ and were baptized.

Perhaps you've heard also about the Great Awakening, the Revival that began in Germany in 1734 in a small Christian Community called Herrnhut. This revival sent out over 300 radical missionaries spreading revival like wildfire to England and then to the United States, resulting in thousands of souls turning to Christ.

Lesser known are the revivals that took place throughout the Civil War. it was during the late Fall of 1863 through the Spring and Summer of 1864 that what was subsequently called the "Great Revival" occurred. Although this event is best documented for Lee's Army of Northern Virginia, it actually took place in both northern and southern armies in both the Virginia and the Tennessee theaters of the war.

According to Confederate Chaplain J. William Jones, virtually every Confederate brigade was affected--and approximately ten percent of the soldiers in the Army of Northern Virginia accepted Christ. Night after night troops participated in worship & prayer meetings. Virtually every gathering ended with soldiers coming forward to accept Christ or receive prayer. When a pond or river was nearby, the soldiers would frequently step forward for baptisms--regardless of how cold the weather was.

U.S. Christian Commission records show that similar events were happening in the North's principle eastern army, the Army of the Potomac, at the same time. Brigade chapels were so full that many men were frequently turned away.

It is estimated that over 100,000 Confederate and somewhere between 100,000 and 200,000 Union troops accepted Christ during the Civil War--roughly ten percent of the men engaged. There are many accounts of the change that took place in the men, both during the war and afterwards, as a result of the many revivals and movement of the Holy Spirit.

In 1904, perhaps the greatest of the modern revivals began in Wales, where over 100,000 were radically converted, transforming society and literally shaking the world with shock waves of revival.

Even today we hear of God's Spirit moving in revival power, in South America, in Cuba and even in China, literally millions of souls are being won for Christ every year

I love to hear stories like that. I love to hear how God's Spirit has moved and is moving, transforming lives and transforming society. Yet, while it is thrilling to hear about revival, my soul has begun to grow impatient with tales of revival at some other time, in some other place, for some other people, and I am growing anxious for a revival here and now. I long for a revival that will rock the world that you and I live in every day.

And I believe it is possible. And I believe God's Word contains the key to revival. While I don't believe there is some formula that we can follow like a magic trick to summon revival, I believe that there are patterns which we can examine to help us understand how to prepare ourselves for revival, to open our hearts and our lives in such a way that God is able to pour out revival at this time and in this place on these people, because I believe that's exactly what God wants to do.

And so, for the next couple of pages I would like for us to look at revival in the Bible, at the stories of some Old Testament Kings. Some stories of revival which will give us some examples to follow; some positive and some not so positive. But before we go to those stories I wanted to look at a powerful passage in Deuteronomy 30. In this passage, the Lord speaks to Israel as they are coming into the land of promise, and he sees a time which Israel will turn away from Him and seeing that time of rebellion God makes a promise of Revival.

He promises that in that time when his people are far away from Him, He will still be willing to draw them near, under certain conditions.

I'd like to look at that promise with you as we begin this quest to find a biblical pattern for revival. The promise begins with...

The Lord's Requirements

1. Remember

"When all these blessings and curses I have set before you come upon you and you take them to heart wherever the LORD your God disperses you among the nations..." (Deut. 30:1 NIV)

That phrase "take them to heart" is more literally translated "call them to mind" or remember. What is the Lord saying here? Well, in the previous chapter he has laid out all the bad things that will happen to Israel if they choose to turn their backs on Him, not as punishment, but simply as natural consequences of their actions. Wars, pestilence, disease, exile from their homeland. Now he is saying, when all those things happen, I want you to remember what I'm saying to you now. I want it to be a wakeup call, I want you to say to yourself, "this is exactly what the Lord said would happen."

He's saying, I want to make things right again, I want to be close to you again, I want revival more than you do but first I need you to *remember*.

It's still true for us today. Perhaps in your life you've wandered far from the Lord, maybe you've never had a relationship with Him at all. You look at your life and it's in shambles, maybe those around you know it and maybe they don't, maybe the circumstances of your life are still holding together and maybe they're falling apart, but inside you're empty. It's time to Remember God's Promise.

Perhaps as a people we have a need to look around at our society – at an entertainment industry that pumps out sewage for our unthinking, uncaring consumption. We need to look at daily interactions among people that have lost in many cases even the semblance of civility. Perhaps it's time to say, "Hey! We don't have to live this way, the Lord said we didn't." Perhaps it's time to remember.

Perhaps even as the local church it's time for us to take a hard look at ourselves. Are we satisfied with where we're at? Are we making a difference in the mission field the Lord has put us in? Are we serving the Lord with all of our heart, soul and mind? Is our gathering on Sunday morning a social ritual or are we committed to making it a Spirit filled celebration and expression of the Body of our Lord Jesus Christ? Perhaps it's time to Remember God's Promise of Revival.

Having remembered, there is a second requirement. God's people must...

2. Return

"...and when you and your children return to the LORD your God and obey him with all your heart and with all your soul according to everything I command you today..." (Deut. 30:2 NIV)

Notice that while obedience to God's Word is expected, a theme we'll see repeated throughout this book, it is not merely an external obedience to the Lord which is required. The emphasis here is internal, with all your heart and with all your soul.

The Lord is saying, when you've come to your senses, turn your heart toward home. Like the Prodigal son, who finally came to his senses in the pig pen, start the journey home, and he's willing to meet us on the road.

When you read verses 6 & 8 it's clear that part of the promise is God's power to enable us to obey His commands, we don't finish the task in our own power but he asks us to start the journey home. The theological word here is repentance--turning from the old way of life. This change of attitude is always at the heart of revival.

In the Welsh Revival of 1904 this transformation of people was the talk of the nation and the world. It was reported that the draft horses of Wales were terribly confused because their drivers would no longer curse and beat them, and the horses simply didn't know what to do!

So, having Remembered the Lord's Promise, we are required to Return to the Lord's Commands. Which Brings us to the second half:

The Lord's Response

1. Restoration

"...then the LORD your God will restore your fortunes and have compassion on you and gather you again from all the nations where he scattered you. 4Even if you have been banished to the most distant land under the heavens, from there the LORD your God will gather you and bring you back. 5He will bring you to the land that belonged to your fathers, and you will take possession of it. He will make you more prosperous and numerous than your fathers..." (Deut. 30:4-5 NIV)

The first thing the Lord does is restore. What had been lost because of sin is restored. The Lord said through the Prophet Joel "I will repay you for the years the locusts have eaten..." (Joel 2:25 NKJV)

Sometimes restoration is simply the natural consequence of our repentance. When we as individuals and as communities begin to live life according to God's plan, things simply begin to work better, and beyond that I believe that God begins to shower his blessings in natural and supernatural ways when we come to him in humility.

Secondly the Lord responds with...

2. Renewal

"The LORD your God will circumcise your hearts and the hearts of your descendants, so that you may love him with all your heart and with all your soul, and live…" (Deut. 30:6 NIV)

Here the emphasis again is internal, and notice how the circle is completed here. In verse two God calls on us to return to Him with all our hearts, here he promises when we do that he will increase the capacity of our hearts to love Him. It is not merely an external return that the Lord is looking for, nor is it merely an external reward of land and riches that he is offering. He is offering the incomparable riches of divine heart surgery, enabling us to love him and serve him.

You say, "well, that's mighty self-serving on His part." No, you see God understands better than anyone that loving and serving him are the reason we were created and so our greatest fulfillment is in the enjoyment of Him.

And when we return to him He sets our hearts free. He renews us for that purpose which we were intended for.

And the last response of the Lord is...

3. Rejoicing

"Then the LORD your God will make you most prosperous in all the work of your hands and in the fruit of your womb, the young of your livestock and the crops of your land. The LORD will again delight in you and make you prosperous, just as he delighted in your fathers…" (Deut. 30:9 NIV)

Here is what's really cool, did you hear it? The rejoicing isn't our rejoicing, IT'S GOD'S!

He rejoices over us! This is why I'm confident that the desire for revival is in sync with God's plan. God rejoices over our return to Him. He's high-fiving the angels; doing the dance of divine delight.

I'm convinced that a lot of the manifestations that accompany many revivals are simply the overflow of God's rejoicing, some of God's joy just spills over onto the objects of his excitement.

Are you like me? Are you ready to stop hearing stories of revival and start living them? Have you looked around at the state of your life, the state of your community, the state of your culture, the state of your chapel and said to yourself, "there must be more"?

Then it's time to *Remember* the Promise of Revival and to *Return* to the Way of the Lord.

The Lord is ready to *Restore* your life, to *Renew* your Heart and He longs to *Rejoice* at your return. In the next chapter, we look at roadblocks to revival.

-Chapter Two-

The Almost Revival

In June of 1995, after years of planning and research costing multiple billions of dollars, the space shuttle Discovery was scheduled to launch for the first of seven missions which would rendezvous with the Russian Space station Mir, in preparation for the launch of the International space station in 1997.

The date had been carefully chosen, weather conditions were favorable but strange noises were coming from Launch Pad 39-B. Upon investigation technicians discovered about six dozen holes in the insulating covering of the main external fuel tank.

All of the complex planning and high priced preparation were useless as the mission ground to a halt because a family of woodpeckers decided that the Space shuttle looked like a good place to live.

The story of Joash is a fascinating one, his was a reign filled with promise. After a steady decline in the kingdom from the time of David a bloody coup had taken place, upon the death of her son the king, Joash's grandmother had killed all of the royal family and set herself upon the throne. But Joash's great aunt had snuck the infant Joash out with his nurse and they hid for six years in a secret place at the Temple of God. When Joash was seven years old the priest Jehoida staged an uprising against the wicked and idolatrous grandmother, placing the boy Joash upon his rightful throne. The temple of Baal in the city was destroyed, the priest of Baal was put to death, the covenant was re-established and proper temple worship was re-established. It looked as if another golden age was coming to the kingdom of Judah. It looked like revival was coming. The plans had been laid, the process had begun but then something went wrong, you could say woodpeckers were discovered in the fuel tank of the revival.

The question for us is, "why?" Why did such a perfect opportunity for revival slip away? What kept God from pouring out his blessing, what did Joash do wrong?

The reason these questions are important to me is that I believe we are in a time that in many ways is similar to the beginning of Joash's reign. A time that looks as if we could be on the brink of revival. Yes, society has experienced moral decline. Yes, terrible things have happened, but there are positive signs, signs that people are growing discontent with the status quo.

So, I think it's important for us to look at the lesson of Joash of almost, but not quite revival. In doing so, we might see the traps to avoid, the things that quench revival. In the story of Joash there are four things that seem to stand out as roadblocks to revival. The first is

"Follow the Leader" Faith.

"Joash did what was right in the eyes of the LORD all the years Jehoiada the priest instructed him." (2 Kings 12:2 NKJV)

"Jehoiada then made a covenant that he and the people and the king would be the LORD'S people." (2 Chron. 23: 16 NKJV)

"After the death of Jehoiada, the officials of Judah came and paid homage to the king, and he listened to them. 18They abandoned the temple of the LORD, the God of their fathers, and worshiped Asherah poles and idols. Because of their guilt, God's anger came upon Judah and Jerusalem." (2 Chron. 24:17-18 NKJV)

As long as Jehoida was around to guide him, Joash did, OK. Not perfect but, OK. But it seems as if there's little conviction in him. It wasn't possible for Jehoida to make a covenant on behalf of the king, the king needed to dedicate himself to the Lord. But I don't believe he ever really did that, and then, as soon as Jehoida is gone, Joash is easily led astray by those who wanted him to turn against the Lord, to reinstate Idol worship and to mix it with the worship of the One true God.

Joash was a follower, and that can be OK if you're a follower with conviction, but Joash seemed to be a follower primarily because He had no convictions.

The same danger exists for us today. It's tempting to follow the crowd or even to follow a charismatic leader, but that's dangerous even when the leader is a good one, because you need to have a personal relationship with the Lord, and if your commitment is leader based it's easy to be led astray or turned around by some other leader. And it's also dangerous because people will let you down. I let people down – ask my wife!

Though we often think of historical revivals in terms of their "leaders"--Jonathan Edwards, D.L. Moody and others, but I don't believe revival has ever come because a leader desired it, but only because the people desired it enough repent of their sin and seek God in prayer with changed hearts and lives. Now a leader may play some part in imparting a vision under God's anointing of what God wants to do, so that the people are inspired to make those changes, but I believe revival has never and will never happen where people seek to ride the coattails of a leader into revival. For that reason, I believe that "follow the leader" faith is a roadblock to revival. The second roadblock is...

Neglecting the Strongholds

"The high places, however, were not removed; the people continued to offer sacrifices and burn incense there." (2 Kings 12:3 NIV)

The high places were centers of idol worship on mountains and hill tops, often poles to the goddess Asherah were erected. Altars, similar to the ones in the temple, for animal and even human sacrifice were often found there.

But they weren't in the cities, and the pagan priests who operated these franchises were often very politically powerful. It sounds as if Joash, once he reached an age where he could have been aware and done something about them, simply wasn't willing to make the effort.

Also remember that idol worship had become more prevalent than genuine worship. The stories in the books of Kings and Chronicles make it clear that many of the kings liked to play both ends of the field--keeping a pagan god on the side just in case the God of Israel didn't come through in a tight spot. To destroy the high places would be to give up your insurance plan.

You may be thinking, what does this have to do with me? I haven't got any high places, we don't worship Idols. Maybe not, but perhaps we do have places hidden in the hills of our lives, places where God is not sovereign, those habits and practicing sins, inappropriate relationships, temptations we indulge, and what about the plans we've made for our lives that we don't want the Lord Messing with. The insurance plan, just in case God doesn't come through. What about your dignity and your reputation? Are you willing for those to be brought low? Are you ready to surrender every corner of your life to God's sovereignty or are you hanging on to the high places.

The story is told of a child who came to school filthy every day, the teachers, appalled that anyone could let their child come to school that way were discussing the situation. One said "that mother doesn't love her child." Another replied, "I think she does, she just doesn't hate dirt." We may say we love the Lord, but until we hate the dirt and tear down the high places, there will be no revival.

The next roadblock to revival is that which should never be surrendered...

Surrender of the Sacred

"About this time Hazael king of Aram went up and attacked Gath and captured it. Then he turned to attack Jerusalem. But Joash king of Judah took all the sacred objects dedicated by his father's—Jehoshaphat, Jehoram and Ahaziah, the kings of Judah—and the gifts he himself had dedicated and all the gold found in the treasuries of the temple of the LORD and of the royal palace, and he sent them to Hazael king of Aram, who then withdrew from Jerusalem." (2 Kings 12:17-18 NKJV)

When faced with a crisis, Joash doesn't turn to the Lord, he doesn't call upon the nation to fast and pray, instead he surrenders the sacred objects, the things dedicated to the Lord. He uses them as a bribe to get his enemy--and the enemy of the Lord to leave him alone. This is another example of Joash's weakness and lack of resolve.

What about us? When push comes to shove in your life what gives way? Is it the things that are sacred to the Lord? When the budget is tight, what gets cut? When something really neat is happening in your local fellowship, where do you find yourself? When your daily schedule is tight does the laundry wait or does the Lord?

The world around us tells us that the sacred has got to go. Bill Gates, Founder and CEO of Microsoft put it this way in an interview "Just in terms of allocation of time resource, religion is not very efficient. There's a lot more I could be doing on a Sunday morning." (Quoted in Chicago Tribune, Jan 13, 1997).

Now, please, don't hear this as some kind of legalism that says you have to "do your time" to be right with the Lord. Galatians is clear that salvation is not based on works or performance. But if we are earnestly seeking a deeper walk with the Lord, if we're hungry for Revival, then all of our resources, time, talent and treasure must belong first to Him, and if we surrender the Sacred for the sake of convenience we shouldn't expect revival.

The last Roadblock comes from 2 Chronicles.

Ignoring the call to Repentance

"Although the LORD sent prophets to the people to bring them back to him, and though they testified against them, they would not listen. Then the Spirit of God came upon Zechariah son of Jehoiada the priest. He stood before the people and said, "This is what God says: 'Why do you disobey the LORD'S commands? You will not prosper. Because you have forsaken the LORD, he has forsaken you.'"

But they plotted against him, and by order of the king they stoned him to death in the courtyard of the LORD'S temple. King Joash did not remember the kindness Zechariah's father Jehoiada had shown him but killed his son, who said as he lay dying, "May the LORD see this and call you to account." (2 Chron. 24:19-22 NKJV)

Even after Joash had strayed far from the path that the Lord had marked out for Him, God in his mercy sent messengers to warn him, to invite him back, to offer revival, restoration. But, Joash didn't want to hear what he was doing was wrong, so he killed the messenger.

I believe it is God's will for us to experience revival--I believe that's always God's will. But I also believe that unless we as individuals and as a community of faith heed the call to repentance we will never experience all that God wants for us. This isn't because God has established a quid pro quo system: You act right and I'll bless you, but simply because the blessing of God and intimacy with Him are simply incompatible with an unrepentant life.

I believe with all my heart that the Lord is willing and anxious to move in revival power in our communities. His plans are made, the shuttle is on the Launch pad. But there are some woodpeckers we need to deal with, the way we deal with them is repentance. Repentance is genuine sorrow for sin--sorrow so genuine that we change our behavior.

I was involved in an 11-day revival that had every opportunity to bust out into what I believed was going to be a mighty outpouring of the Spirit of God. Sadly, on night number 10 the Holy Spirit was grieved because some of these roadblocks had not been dealt with.

Don't miss your time of visitation! Deal with the roadblock now!

-Chapter Three-

Tearing Down the High Places

In one of the houses I grew up in we had an ongoing encounter with some pests that had the endearing name of "sewer flies." Exterminators repeatedly came and each time the flies would disappear for a while, only to return a few weeks later.

As it turned out there was a bigger problem than sewer flies--the sewer flies were merely a symptom of the leak in the drain under our kitchen. This leak resulted in a damp warm spot in our crawls space that was a perfect breeding ground for the flies. The fly problem was finally solved when the leak was fixed and the breeding ground was taken away.

In the last chapter, we talked about Joash and how his promising reign fell short of its promise because he failed to get rid of the high places, those places of pagan worship hidden in the hills, the breeding grounds for all sorts of evil activity.

In this chapter, we are treated to the example of Hezekiah, a king whom the Bible says, "did what was right in the eyes of the LORD."

As we looked at Joash, we asked ourselves what went wrong, what was it about Joash's reign that kept the Lord from sending revival. Now we want to ask ourselves, what went right? What was it about Hezekiah's reign that found favor in God's eyes and led to revival?

I think that the answer to that question is fairly straightforward, I see three very specific things in this eight verse summary of Hezekiah's reign that give us a clear indication of what it was about Hezekiah that pleased God. The first is in verse four, and it is His complete...

Turnaround

"He removed the high places, smashed the sacred stones and cut down the Asherah poles. He broke into pieces the bronze snake Moses had made, for up to that time the Israelites had been burning incense to it." (2 Kings 18:4 NKJV)

Joash, failed to tear down the high places. He wasn't willing to make the effort to confront those strongholds of sin and idolatry; and the consequence was that the momentum toward revival was overcome by the evil of those strongholds, both in the nation and in Joash himself.

Hezekiah on the other hand doesn't fool around in his turnaround. He takes reform all the way to the hills. He confronts the pagan priests and idolaters. He says, there is no room for this kind of activity in my kingdom, because my kingdom is really God's kingdom. There aren't going to be parts of this kingdom that don't bow down to His authority--He will be Lord of All.

If we want to experience revival in our lives, in our homes, in our church, in our community we're going to have to make the same bold stand. We cannot afford to have holdouts. We cannot allow the high places of sin to escape the Lord's authority. We can't say "Lord you can have all of my life except--my finances, my relationships, my entertainment, my plans."

Historically revival has come to the church when people have allowed the Holy spirit to take the jackhammer of repentance to the strongholds of their lives and once those barriers are broken, the river of revival comes crashing through.

Yes, the river sweeps through with blessing, and the story of Hezekiah's reign demonstrates that, the enemies of God's people are overcome, but the first step is repentance. Simply put, the first step is *turnaround*.

The second thing about Hezekiah that pleased God and led to revival was his complete...

Trust

"Hezekiah trusted in the LORD, the God of Israel. There was no one like him among all the kings of Judah, either before him or after him." (2 Kings 18:5 NIV)

Hezekiah, the Bible says, trusted in the Lord and note that it is this trust in the Lord which leads the author of the biblical record to comment that there was no other king like him among all the others before and after who had sat in that throne.

Hezekiah's forefather, David declared "Some trust in chariots and some in horses, but we trust in the name of the LORD our God. They are brought to their knees and fall, but we rise up and stand firm." (Ps. 20:7-8)

It must be easy for a king to trust in the resources of His kingdom, to try to devise a way to solve their problems with weapons or wisdom or wealth, the way that Joash did, but Hezekiah trusted in the Lord.

Without faith, the Book of Hebrews says, it is impossible to please God. But as we see here, with faith and trust in the Lord, God is genuinely pleased.

If we are ever going to please the Lord, He will require of us the same that he required of Kings of Judah: repentance & faith or turnaround and trust.

First that trust must mean trusting in Him for salvation; believing that the sacrifice of Christ upon the cross is sufficient to pay the price for your sins and to make you right before God. This is the foundation of a God-blessed life.

Then when that central issue of salvation is dealt with the Lord wants us to trust him with more, with all of our life. He wants us to rely upon him for deliverance from the enemy, for daily bread, for our families and our future.

Dr. G. Campbell Morgan said this about believers who are reluctant to commit themselves wholeheartedly to Christ: "When our convictions are yielded to Him completely, He is able to give Himself to us in all His fullness. Until that is so, He cannot trust us. How true it is that we often miss the joy and strength of our Christianity because, by withholding ourselves from Christ, we make it impossible for Him to give Himself to us in all the fullness of His grace and truth." (Today in the Word, April 1998, p. 23)

You see in this way we give ourselves completely to Him, by trusting Him with all our lives, and when we do that we open ourselves up to His blessing, not that He's been withholding it but simply that we have been unable to receive it. So then with TRUST as with TURNAROUND we open the floodgates of revival.

There is one final thing about Hezekiah that the Scripture is careful to note and I think it's an important point for us too. The last thing about Hezekiah that pleased God and opened the way for revival was Hezekiah's...

Tenacity

"He held fast to the LORD and did not cease to follow him; he kept the commands the LORD had given Moses. And the LORD was with him; he was successful in whatever he undertook. He rebelled against the king of Assyria and did not serve him." (2 Kings 18:6-7 NKJV)

Hezekiah stuck to it. It wasn't that he never faced difficulty but unlike Josiah who when faced with a crisis surrendered what was sacred, Hezekiah plunged forward with unwavering commitment, he continued to trust and he continued to do what was right even when confronted by the world's only superpower of his day. Even when he saw the neighboring northern kingdom of Israel defeated and sent off into exile, he continued to serve God in faith and righteousness.

And if we are genuine in our desire to see God moving in our lives in a new and a fresh way, if we long to see His blessing, we must exhibit the same kind of spiritual tenacity.

If I had to guess the number one reason why revival doesn't come at times and places where it seems as if revival is likely I would say it is the lack of tenacity. I have seen time and again and perhaps you have too, people who are anxious for God to move in power, people who earnestly desire to have a new vision and deeper understanding of the majesty and holiness of God, people who are anxious to see the lost come to faith, people who believe they have a God given vision for revival, people who have begun special prayer meetings to ask God to send revival but who never seem to get there, Oh I don't mean to say nothing happens--there is always spiritual fruit when people desire to draw closer to the Lord. But you know what I mean, the outcome never quite lives up to the expectation.

Why does that happen? I don't know for sure--perhaps part of it is simply our inability to box God and to define what revival is going to look like. But I suspect that part of it is the lack of this one thing on our part: *tenacity*.

After a few weeks, the attendance at prayer meetings begins to dwindle. After a few times inviting our friends and neighbors to church, we quit asking. After a few days of resisting temptation, we give in.

In 1913 in the French Alps, because of careless deforestation, the mountains around Provence, France were barren. Former villages were deserted because their springs and brooks had run dry. The wind blew furiously, unimpeded by foliage. A simple shepherd named Elzeard Bouffier, took it upon himself to do something about it. Each night he meticulously sorted through a pile of acorns, discarding those that were cracked or undersized. When the shepherd had counted out 100 perfect acorns, he stopped for the night and went to bed. By 1913, the 55-year-old shepherd had been planting trees on the wild hillsides for over three years. He had planted 1,100,000 trees, 20,000 of which had sprouted. Of those, he expected half to be eaten by rodents or die to the elements, and the other half to live.

By the middle of the century something incredible had happened: there was a veritable forest, accompanied by a chain reaction in nature. Water flowed in the once-empty brooks. The ecology, sheltered by a leafy roof and bonded to the earth by a mat of spreading roots, become hospitable. Willows, rushes, meadows, gardens, and flowers were birthed. Where there had been only ruins now stand neat farms. Little by little, the villages have been rebuilt. (Hal Seed, Oceanside, California, Leadership, Spring, 1993, p. 48)

What brought about the transformation? The *tenacity* of one simple farmer. We began with an illustration about sewer flies, and how the only way to rid yourself of them is to deny them a breeding ground. We conclude with this illustration about reestablishing habitat. The two are really two sides of the same coin--much like the lives of Joash and Hezekiah. Each of us today must choose which type habitat we will nurture.

To choose life we must choose to *turn around*, and tear down the high places giving God sovereignty over every part of our life, leaving no breeding ground for temptation and sin. And we must choose to trust in Christ alone, both for salvation from sin and its penalty and for all that matters in our lives. And it cannot be just a temporary decision we must choose to follow hard after the Lord with *tenacity*.

-Chapter Four-

Just a little more Time

In 1912, the "unsinkable" Titanic was launched in Liverpool, England. So haughty was the hoopla surrounding the Titanic's safety and structural integrity that it caused dismay among some of the God fearing public. Such pride was exemplified, many felt it was tempting God to show man his folly. And while it's certainly not our place 100 years later to say that what happened when the ship met the iceberg was God's answer to the pride of the ship's builders and promoters, we do know for certain that their pride was misplaced and the "unsinkable ship" took 1500 lives with it to the bottom of the ocean.

The Titanic was one famous case of pride coming before a fall. Less known to us today but probably of greater spiritual benefit is the case of Hezekiah at the end of His life. In the last chapter, you read about the revival of Hezekiah; of how his life and reign pleased the Lord and how the Lord responded by pouring out his blessings, how the Lord visited his people in revival power because of the king's faithful leadership.

Here at the end of Hezekiah's life are several lessons we would do well to learn if we hope to see the Lord move in revival power among us.

Two of the lessons are encouragements and two are cautions. The first is a word of encouragement as we see God continue to pour out his blessings upon Hezekiah, this lesson has to do with...

The Power of Prayer

"In those days Hezekiah became ill and was at the point of death. He prayed to the LORD, who answered him and gave him a miraculous sign." (2 Chron. 32:24 NKJV)

Hezekiah receives the word of the Lord from the prophet Isaiah that he is going to die, but Hezekiah calls out to the Lord for mercy and the Lord answers his prayer not only with healing but with a miraculous sign, literally making the sun go backwards in the sky.

The lesson is clear for us even today, we serve a God who answers prayer, and answers miraculously. You say those are just Bible stories, things like that don't happen anymore. Try to explain that to a little boy I prayed for in New Zealand who was born with crooked legs. He had never been able to run in his entire life. Yet, after praying for just a few short moments he began running up and down the aisles weeping!

God answers prayer today like He did in Hezekiah's time. If you have a need bring it to the Lord in Prayer, he wants to hear your needs and he wants you to trust Him for the answer, there is Power in Prayer.

Well that's an encouragement so how about a caution? The second lesson is about

The Problem of Pride

"But Hezekiah's heart was proud and he did not respond to the kindness shown him; therefore the LORD'S wrath was on him and on Judah and Jerusalem." (2 Chron. 32:25 NKJV)

After Hezekiah's miraculous healing, which came after His miraculous victory over the ancient World's only superpower, Hezekiah develops a problem, the problem of pride. When the king of Babylon sends "messengers" with a get well gift he invites them in and shows them not only all of his wealth but all of his weaponry, as if to say to them, "this is how we defeated the king of Assyria."

The moral of this story? Not only are those who have been blessed by God not immune from the trap of pride, they are probably more susceptible to it.

The great British preacher Charles Spurgeon was keenly aware of the dangers of pride. After his sermon one Sunday, Spurgeon was met by a woman who exclaimed, "Oh, Mr. Spurgeon, that was wonderful." "Yes, madam," Spurgeon replied, "so the devil whispered in my ear as I came down the steps of the pulpit."(Today in the Word, February 27, 1997, p. 34)

Spurgeon understood that God's blessings wrongly construed as our own accomplishments is dangerous territory. One reason the enemy uses this trick so often is that it is so successful.

When you have been blessed by God, Beware the Problem of Pride. Be quick to give glory to God for his blessings, Be not anxious to draw attention to self, because pride indeed does come before a fall.

The third lesson is another encouragement.

The Promise to the Prodigal

"Then Hezekiah repented of the pride of his heart, as did the people of Jerusalem; therefore the LORD'S wrath did not come upon them..." (2 Chron. 32: 26a NIV)

Once again the Prophet Isaiah plays a key role in the story. He confronts Hezekiah with His pride and Hezekiah, along with the nation repents and true to His word as we read just a few chapters back in Deuteronomy 30, when His people repent, God is anxious to receive them back.

Never let the enemy deceive You that you are outside the reach of God's grace. If you have drifted far from the Lord, because of pride or even because of willful sin or just plain negligence, The Lord is calling you home to fellowship with Him. Like the Father of the prodigal son, he longs to restore you, but first you must return in faith and repentance to Him. And as the text indicates this is both an individual and a corporate need. Perhaps the most eloquent call for corporate repentance I've seen outside the Scripture was the one offered by President Abraham Lincoln in his Proclamation of a Day of National Humiliation, Fasting and Prayer, 1863

"We have been the recipients of the choicest bounties of heaven; we have been preserved these many years in peace and prosperity; we have grown in numbers, wealth, and power as no other nation has ever grown. But we have forgotten God. We have forgotten the gracious hand which preserved us in peace and multiplied and enriched and strengthened us, and we have vainly imagined, in the deceitfulness of our hearts, that all these blessings were produced by some superior wisdom and virtue of our own. Intoxicated with unbroken success, we have become too self-sufficient to feel the necessity of redeeming and preserving grace, too proud to pray to the God that made us.

Yes we as a nation we as a church have a need to confess our collective pride and like the prodigal return home humbled before our father, who longs to give us a share in His blessings."

The final lesson is again a caution.

The Price of Pride

"...therefore the LORD'S wrath did not come upon them during the days of Hezekiah." (2 Chron. 32:26b NKJV)

They say that the chickens always come home to roost, and I don't know exactly what that means because my chicken experience is somewhat limited but I do know this: Sin has consequences and pride is one of the most basic forms of sin. There is a price to be paid for pride. Though the Lord relented during the time of Hezekiah, his sin of pride in sharing his secrets with the Babylonians is the first step toward the eventual defeat and exile of Judah and the humiliation of the line of David.

Is this God's punishment? Perhaps, but part of it can be chalked up to natural consequences of sin. You show the enemy what you've got and the enemy gets you.

Our sin and our pride reaps a crop too, sometimes immediate and sometimes down the road. Like Mad cow disease, you may have ate that burger yesterday and feel fine today, but the consequences are brewing and 6-30 years down the road the payment comes due.

Sometimes we see this with physical consequences in our bodies--the drunkard will pay a price. Sometimes like Hezekiah it is visited upon future generations, how's that you say? One way is that our dedication or lack thereof is affecting the formation of our children. The emphasis you place on serving the Lord will be seen in them, if you are lax in your commitment, don't be surprised when your children are doubly lax.

I mentioned as we began that before the Titanic sailed on its ill-fated maiden voyage, that many Christians were distressed at the haughtiness of the advertising of the ship's invulnerability. This was particularly true of one God-fearing woman, whose family was unexpectedly transferred onto the gigantic liner for its maiden voyage. After reading the shipbuilders' claims, Mrs. Hart believed—and so stated—"This is flying in the face of God!" The woman's daughter Eva Hart, 7 at the time of the voyage, recalls that her family was saved from tragedy because of Mrs. Hart's spiritual convictions. Throughout the voyage, Mrs. Hart stayed awake at night waiting for disaster to strike, and thus was able to move her family to an upper deck almost immediately after the ship collided with an unseen iceberg. Because of her vigilance, the family did not join the 1,500 others who died that night. (Today in the Word, July, 1989, p. 8)

How vigilant are you? Having experienced the blessings of a gracious God, are you in danger of experiencing the shipwreck of pride?

-Chapter Five-

Wasted Years

On Friday 14th April, 1999, Wall Street experienced its biggest one-day fall in history, ending a week in which US markets lost $2 trillion in value — the equivalent to Germany's entire economy. Virtually all of the losses came in the Information Technology sector and what had been called the "dotcom bubble" became the "dotcom crash." Bill Gates saw his personal fortune drop $30 billion in a few hours. In the following months more than 430 Internet companies closed up shop and 100, 000 people lost their jobs. Oh how the mighty have fallen.

What's the point? Things can change suddenly. Even when everything looks peachy they can go bad quickly as a result of carelessness or misconduct. In spite of a brief downturn as the result of pride, things were going well in the nation of Judah spiritually and materially under Hezekiah's rule. God was responding to his people's repentance and faithfulness with revival blessing.

Now we look at what happens when Hezekiah's son Manasseh takes over the kingdom. And the picture is not good--we could call it anti-revival.

You might be thinking why look at this in a book on revival? The answer is because it's a part of the story and it's included for a reason. It's a big flashing warning light to us: "don't let this happen to you."

As I look at the story of Manasseh's reign my response is primarily sadness, this is a sad chapter in Israel's history and Manasseh's is a sad life.

I'd like us to look at that life and be cautioned as we are meant to be. The first thing that makes Manasseh's reign sad is that he..

DEPARTED from the Faith of his Father

"He rebuilt the high places his father Hezekiah had demolished; he also erected altars to the Baals and made Asherah poles. He bowed down to all the starry hosts and worshiped them." (2 Chron. 33:3 NIV)

You'll remember that the high places are a recurring theme. Several promising times saw revival thwarted by the unwillingness of the kings and the people to tear down the high places. Finally in the reign of Hezekiah, they came down, we can only assume at great cost.

Now upon Hezekiah's death what does Mannaseh do? He not only allows them to be rebuilt, he apparently is one of the principal users. In fact he becomes involved in every imaginable idolatrous and occult practice including witchcraft and the sacrifice of his own son to idols. I'd say that's a big departure and I'd say that's pretty sad.

Perhaps you have been blessed with a Godly heritage. Be protective of it. It's easy to look upon that heritage as old fashioned and belonging to another age, but our parents, spiritual and natural, learned at great cost that the high places were not to be trifled with. That you can't live a life that's pleasing to the Lord in isolation from the church, that you can't just visit the enemy's territory for entertainment occasionally, and that to try to do so leaves you vulnerable to the attacks of the enemy without a protective covering.

If you depart from the faith of your fathers you're headed for destruction too. The second thing that's sad about Manasseh's reign is that he...

DEFILED the Temple of the Lord

"He built altars in the temple of the LORD, of which the LORD had said, "My Name will remain in Jerusalem forever." In both courts of the temple of the LORD, he built altars to all the starry hosts." (2 Chron. 33:4-5 NKJV)

The temple was God's special place, set apart sanctified for him. Manasseh not only let idol worship take place on the hillsides, he brought it right into God's special place.

In the New Testament were told that because of the work of Christ we ourselves have become the temple, in fact that our bodies are the temple of the Holy Spirit.

I imagine that some of you would be offended if we brought the dumpster from outside and dumped it on your living room floor. Yet how often have we been guilty of letting worse filth into the real temple?

The third thing that makes Manasseh's reign sad is that he...

DECEIVED the People of God

"But Manasseh led Judah and the people of Jerusalem astray, so that they did more evil than the nations the LORD had destroyed before the Israelites." (2 Chron. 33:9)

People look to their leaders for instruction and example. In corrupting his own life, Manasseh was responsible also for the corruption of God's people. Bad company corrupts good morals. (1 Cor. 15:33)

Josiah Wedgwood, English maker of the famous Wedgwood pottery, was showing a nobleman through his factory one day. One of Wedgwood's employees, a young boy, was accompanying them. The nobleman was profane and vulgar. At first, the boy was shocked by his irreverence; then he became fascinated by the man's coarse jokes and laughed at them.

Wedgwood was deeply distressed. At the conclusion of the tour, he showed the nobleman a vase of unique design. The man was charmed by its exquisite shape and rare beauty. As he reached for it, Mr. Wedgwood purposely let it fall to the floor. The nobleman uttered an angry oath and said, "I wanted that vase for my collection, and you have ruined it by your carelessness!" Wedgwood answered, "Sir, there are other ruined things more precious than a vase which can never be restored. You can never give back to that young man, who just left us, the reverence for sacred things which his parents have tried to teach him for years. You have undone their labor in less than half an hour!" (Morning Glory, Sept.-Oct., 1997, p. 32)

You say, "Well I'm not a leader, no one is looking at me. What I do is my business." Each of us is a leader to someone, our family our children our friends, our enemies who are looking to see with what kind of conviction we live our lives before God and man, and we are responsible for the effect that our lives lived out before them affect the decisions they make. And if we show them by our behavior that God's expectations are unimportant then we are deceiving them.

The fourth sad fact of Manasseh's reign is that he...

DISREGARDED the Word of the Lord

"The LORD spoke to Manasseh and his people, but they paid no attention." (2 Chron. 33:10 NIV)

The Lord in His mercy called out to the king and the people to come back to Him. But Manasseh turned a deaf ear. Tradition tells us that Manasseh was the king who was responsible for the death of the Prophet Isaiah, sawing him in two with a wood saw. Why? Because he tired of hearing God's call to repentance, like a broken record.

Ronald Reagan as a young man worked at a radio station and sometimes played records of sermons, sometimes he would set the record to play in the one man operation and sneak out for a cup of coffee. One day he got a call at the coffee shop from the stations owner telling him to get back to the station now and after that night he was fired. He returned to the station to find the record skipping "Go to hell, go to hell..."

God's call to repentance can sound like that, but the broken record is the loving voice of God's mercy, offering us the chance not only for salvation but for genuine blessing and revival.

The last sad thing about Josiah's reign is ...

DELAYED His Surrender to the Lord

"Manasseh was twelve years old when he became king, and he reigned in Jerusalem fifty-five years. He did evil in the eyes of the LORD, following the detestable practices of the nations the LORD had driven out before the Israelites." (2 Chron. 33:1-2 NKJV)

"So the LORD brought against them the army commanders of the king of Assyria, who took Manasseh prisoner, put a hook in his nose, bound him with bronze shackles and took him to Babylon. 12In his distress he sought the favor of the LORD his God and humbled himself greatly before the God of his fathers. 13And when he prayed to him, the LORD was moved by his entreaty and listened to his plea; so he brought him back to Jerusalem and to his kingdom. Then Manasseh knew that the LORD is God." (2 Chron. 33:11-13 NIV)

You might be thinking "How can this be sad? He came back to the Lord." And my answer is that he came too late and he wasted too much time and opportunity.

The writers of the books of Kings and Chronicles were trained in the Army Writing style. They always give us the bottom line up front and they give to each king one of two evaluations, either "He did right in the eyes of the Lord," or "He did evil in the eyes of the LORD." Manasseh gets the second. In spite of the fact that he repents at the end of his life. This troubled me for a while. In fact, I used to have conversations with friends where I would question, why does he get the "evil" stamp when he ended up returning to the Lord and being restored? And then I read that Manasseh had the longest reign of any king of Israel or Judah. He had more opportunity to do good than any other king. Yet for almost all of that time He chose what was wrong and he only finally changed when God in his mercy allowed him to be bound in chains and dragged to Babylon with a hook in his nose--yes this was God's version of tough love and finally it worked but at what cost and after how much had been wasted. Douglas MacArthur said, in war all tragedy can be summarized in two words, "too late."

What about you how long will you wait? God has given you life and the opportunity to serve Him. That gift is like this beautiful bouquet, what will you do with it? Will you waste your life worshipping at the high places of illicit pleasure saying "oh there's still time?"

Will you allow God's Temple, your body, to be defiled by the filth of the world and tell yourself "Oh, I'll clean that later?"

Will you by your example cause the lives of others to be destroyed in the process?

Will you yet again today disregard the pleading voice of the Lord to return, saying still, "tomorrow, tomorrow?"

Will you waste even more God given opportunity to live a life filled with genuine pleasure making a positive difference in the World as an instrument in the hands of God. Will you squander your life until you finally hit the bottom in chains dragged around by Satan's hook through your nose?

Will you then turn to God and say "Here's what's left of my life, God, I'll give you the stalks?"

-Chapter Six-

Too Young for Revival?

Hattie May Wiatt lived near a church where the Sunday School was very crowded. One day the pastor, Russel Conwell, found her crying outside the building because there was no room inside and he told her that one day when they had raised enough money they would have buildings big enough to allow everyone to attend who wanted to. Not long after that Hattie May became sick and died. Rev. Conwell was asked to do the funeral and the girl's mother told him that Hattie May had been saving money to help build a bigger church and gave him the little purse in which she had saved 57 cents.

This was in 1886 when 57 cents was no small savings account for a little girl from a poor family. Rev. Conwell had the 57 cents turned into 57 pennies, told the congregation the story of little Hattie May and sold the pennies for a return of about $250. In addition, 54 of the original 57 pennies were returned to Rev. Conwell and he later put them up on display. Some of the members of the church formed what they called the Wiatt Mite Society which was dedicated to making Hattie May's 57 cents grow as much as possible and to buy the property for the Primary Department of the Sunday school. A house nearby was purchased with the $250 that Hattie May's 57 cents had produced. The first classes of Temple College, later Temple University, were held in that house. It was later sold to allow Temple College to move and the growth of Temple, along with the founding of the Good Samaritan Hospital (now the Temple University Hospital) along with the 3500 seat auditorium of Temple Baptist Church serve as powerful testimonies to the leadership of a little girl named Hattie May.

It's easy when you're young to suppose that making a big impact in the world is something for those who are older. That if the Lord did happen to have big plans for your life, that those plans are on hold waiting for adulthood.

But, throughout the pages of Scripture some of the Lord's greatest victories are led by the young. The young man Joseph in spite of imprisonment and slavery saved both his family and the rest of the world from starvation. Samuel heard the Lord call his name when he was still a child. Only a boy named David defeated the Philistine champion Goliath. History's Messiah was delivered to us by a girl named Mary who yielded herself to God's plan and named her baby Jesus.

And here at the end of 2 Chronicles we read about a boy named Josiah who led his nation Judah in its last great revival.

I believe it is and always has been God's plan to use young people to forcefully move forward his plan.

Even in my own experience I have seen the young people of a church get on fire for God and lead the church into revival.

The question is how can young people and older people alike make a difference for the Lord?

I think that a key or a pattern is found in the life of Josiah. I'd like to look at three things Josiah did which I believe led to revival. The first thing is that Josiah...

I. Sought the Lord

"In the eighth year of his reign, while he was still young, he began to seek the God of his father David…" (2 Chron. 34:3a NKJV)

At a certain point in time Josiah made a decision to seek the God of his fathers. Perhaps it was a decision that had been brewing for a while, but the text makes note that it was when he was 16 years old that he began to seek the Lord. He began to be dissatisfied with the status quo. He was unwilling to let things stay the way that they were.

Somewhere inside of him the way things were didn't seem right, somewhere inside of him he longed for truth. He began to recognize that God shaped hole in his heart and he determined to fill it. Whether in the young or in the old, revival always begins when individuals recognize the interior call of God and that longing gives way to an earnest seeking.

In the book of Jeremiah the Lord tells his people that a time is coming when everything comfortable will be stripped away and that in that time they will seek the Lord and that they will find him when they seek Him with all of their hearts. I believe Josiah found himself in just such a time, and I believe that he did seek the Lord with all of his heart and that God was there waiting to be found.

You see it's not God who hides from us, but we who hide from God. But when our heart recognizes his gentle call he rejoices to see us seeking him.

This inward stirring that leads to outward seeking is one of the first steps to revival. Josiah sought the Lord and when he had found the Lord he...

II. Started the Process

"...In his twelfth year he began to purge Judah and Jerusalem of high places, Asherah poles, carved idols and cast images." (2 Chron. 34:3b NKJV)

In his seeking of the Lord Josiah began to understand that his life and his kingdom wasn't measuring up to God's expectations and so he decided to do something about it.

Of course we know that outward obedience is not God's primary desire from us. What he desires is that we trust in Him, and for us today, since Christ has died for our sins, the Lord wants us to trust him for salvation first and foremost. With that trusting comes a changed heart and a changed attitude that desires to please God – not to earn his favor but out of gratitude for his love. I think this is the change that we see in Josiah as he begins to purge the kingdom of Idol worship.

Now think about it, this couldn't have been an easy decision, Josiah had significant obstacles to overcome.

First his Age. I'm sure there were those around who questioned such a bold stand by such a young man, there were probably those who laughed it off as the folly of youth--a little guy with a big plan that would soon be gathering dust like so many unfinished projects in a teenager's closet. But Josiah had heard the Lord's voice and he carried on regardless of what anyone said.

secondly there was the obstacle of his Background. Both his father and grandfather had been known as wicked kings. He hadn't been raised in a godly home. Young person and old person alike, even if you don't have Christian parents or relatives, you can still be used mightily by God.

Thirdly there was the obstacle of the crowd. The nation of Judah was thoroughly ungodly. Josiah was swimming upstream in a big way. But he had had a vision of God and of God's plan and he didn't need the encouragement of the crowd to do what was right. He was willing to stand alone and he started the process of putting the vision into practice regardless of what the crowd said or thought or did.

The last thing that Josiah did to bring on revival was that he...

III. Smashed the Idols

The thing I'm getting at here is the thoroughness of Josiah's housecleaning. Read the passage and see if you don't think that the Scripture is trying to make a point here.

"In his twelfth year he began to purge Judah and Jerusalem of high places, Asherah poles, carved idols and cast images. Under his direction the altars of the Baals were torn down; he cut to pieces the incense altars that were above them, and smashed the Asherah poles, the idols and the images. These he broke to pieces and scattered over the graves of those who had sacrificed to them. He burned the bones of the priests on their altars, and so he purged Judah and Jerusalem. In the towns of Manasseh, Ephraim and Simeon, as far as Naphtali, and in the ruins around them, he tore down the altars and the Asherah poles and crushed the idols to powder and cut to pieces all the incense altars throughout Israel. Then he went back to Jerusalem." (2 Chron. 34:3-7 NIV)

You know, maybe it's just me, but I think burning the bones of the priests and crushing the idols to powder is a pretty extreme response. It's a graphic illustration of the act of repentance--turning away from sin and forcefully rooting out every root and reminder of its presence.

What if I offered you some brownies and told you they were my secret recipe brownies. You just add one cup of dog poop to the mix? You'd look at me funny--how would you feel about a half cup of dog poop? A Tablespoon? A Teaspoon? Well exactly how much dog poop is acceptable in brownies?

The point is that there are some things that there is no acceptable level of. Sin is one of those things.

Josiah recognized that he not only needed to close down the pagan altars but that every reminder of their presence needed to be utterly destroyed.

It's not OK to have just a little bit of sin for extra spice in your life. In any quantity sin that we willingly allow in our lives gives the enemy of our souls a foothold.

We squirm at the thought of eating my special recipe brownies, but willingly ingest the putrid filth of the world that is far more dangerous to us. Jesus said to the Pharisees who were so concerned about hand washing but who spewed hateful conversation from their mouths: "What goes into a man's mouth does not make him 'unclean,' but what comes out of his mouth, that is what makes him 'unclean.'" (Matthew 15:11 AMP)

If we genuinely long to make a difference in the world, or in our church, we like Josiah must not be content to simply pull down the Asherah poles but we must smash the idols to powder.

Hattie May Wiatt made a difference because she caught sight of a vision and she decided to take action.

What about you? Do you have a vision of what God can do in and through you?

Have you begun to Seek the Lord with all of your heart?

Have you followed through with the decision to begin the process? Have you gotten the ball rolling with a bold stand for Jesus Christ?

Are you willing to Smash the idols and empty your life of every stronghold of the enemy?

-Chapter Seven-

Hey! What's this book?

At the Gold City Gem Mine in Franklin, North Carolina customers pay a small fee for a "bucket of dirt" out of the mine. The dirt contains rocks, usually worthless, the joy of treasure hunting and occasionally a real gemstone out of the mine. In July of 1995, a third-grader name Griffin McCurry, paid for just such a bucket of dirt. As you might expect it didn't look as if there was any hidden treasure, but there was a rock in it that the boy kept just because he liked the shape. People magazine reported that it was a saleswoman from the Jewelry store at the mine who noticed the rock and gave it a closer inspection. As it turned out the 1104 carat sapphire had a value of approximately $45,000.

Everybody likes a good treasure story, and the story of the discovery of the Law in the Temple during Josiah's renovation is about as good as they come, because God's word is a treasure that is priceless.

But this is more than just a story of lost and found, this is a story about God choosing to reveal himself. The Law wasn't just found accidentally, God chose to reveal his Word, which is to say that God chose to reveal himself to Josiah and the nation he led. God could have made that choice at any time in the previous kings' reigns, yet he chose to reveal it Josiah

The question we need to ask ourselves is why Josiah? What did he do that caused the Lord to draw near to him in this special way.

We have been talking about the topic of revival, and what happens here in Josiah's reign is what revival is all about: God showing himself to his people. The people of God having a fresh revelation or more precisely a fresh understanding of the person and work of Jesus Christ. That comes by God's choice not ours but I think that we can see in this story a couple of the things that Josiah did that made God decide to reveal himself anew during the time of Josiah. As usual I'm looking for an intentional Biblical pattern here that we can put into practice here and now. So let's look first at what was going on when the discovery was made, Josiah was...

I. Working--doing what he knew was right

"In the eighteenth year of his reign, King Josiah sent the secretary, Shaphan son of Azaliah, the son of Meshullam, to the temple of the LORD. He said: "Go up to Hilkiah the high priest and have him get ready the money that has been brought into the temple of the LORD, which the doorkeepers have collected from the people. Have them entrust it to the men appointed to supervise the work on the temple. And have these men pay the workers who repair the temple of the LORD—6the carpenters, the builders and the masons. Also have them purchase timber and dressed stone to repair the temple." (2 Kings 22:3-7 NIV)

Josiah's folks didn't just happen upon the Book of the Law in the street somewhere. They were in God's house doing housecleaning. They were positioned to find that book because Josiah had looked at the Lord's house and said it was a disgrace. He'd decided that it was time to do some repairs. He was seeking to honor God by repairing the temple.

Friends if we're going to see revival in the here and now it's not going to be because we stumble upon it somewhere, but because we're busy doing what we know is right, because we are honoring God with our lives. Sure our knowledge might not be complete and there might be some more things the Lord will require of us when He draws near, just like he did in Josiah's time but he'll give us that specific stuff when he sees we're doing the general stuff. Why? Because it demonstrates we have an appreciation for his word and an intent to follow through.

A story is told of a man who loved old books. He met an acquaintance who had just thrown away a Bible that had been stored in the attic of his ancestral home for generations. "I couldn't read it," the friend explained. "Somebody named Guten-something had printed it." "Not Gutenberg!" the book lover exclaimed in horror. "That Bible was one of the first books ever printed. Why, a copy just sold for over two million dollars!" His friend was unimpressed. "Mine wouldn't have brought a dollar. Some fellow named Martin Luther had scribbled all over it in German."

The man didn't have an appreciation of what he had. But Josiah by his working to do what he knew to do, demonstrated an appreciation for the things of the Lord. The second reason I believe God chose to reveal his Word to Josiah was that Josiah was...

II. Willing to do what the Lord asked

"Then Shaphan the secretary informed the king, "Hilkiah the priest has given me a book." And Shaphan read from it in the presence of the king. 11When the king heard the words of the Book of the Law, he tore his robes." (2 Kings 22:10-11 NKJV)

Here again we see Josiah as a man with a repentant heart, willing when he saw the wrong to turn toward the right. He shows he's willing to follow the Lord. Why should the Lord choose to reveal himself to us in a special way if we have not demonstrated a willingness to follow?

Frederick Charrington was a member of the wealthy family in England which owned the Charrington Brewery. His personal fortune, derived solely from his brewing enterprise, exceeded $66 million.

One night, Charrington was walking along a London street with a few friends. Suddenly the door of a pub flew open just a few steps ahead of the group, and a man staggered out into the street with a woman clinging desperately to him. The man, obviously very drunk, was swearing at the woman and trying to push her away. The woman was gaunt and clad in rags. She sobbed and pleaded with the drunken man, who was her husband. "Please, dear, please!" she cried as Charrington and his friends watched. "The children haven't eaten in two days! And I've not eaten in a week! For the love of God, please come home! Or if you must stay, just give me a few coins so I can buy the children some..." Her pleas were brutally cut off as her husband struck her a savage blow. She collapsed to the stone pavement like a rag doll. The man stood over her with his fists clenched, poised as if to strike her again. Charrington leaped forward and grasped him. The man struggled, swearing violently, but Charrington pinned the man's arms securely behind his back. Charrington's companions rushed to the woman's side and began ministering to her wounds. A short time later a policeman led the drunken man away and the woman was taken to a nearby hospital.

As Charrington brushed himself off, he noticed a lighted sign in the window of the pub: "Drink Chrarrington Ale." The multi-millionaire brewer was suddenly shaken to the core of his being. He realized that his confrontation with the violent husband would not have happened if the man's brain had not been awash with the Charrington family's product. "When I saw that sign," he later wrote, "I was stricken just as surely as Paul on the Damascus Road. Here was the source of my family wealth, and it was producing untold human misery before my own eyes. Then and there I pledged to God that not another penny of that money should come to me."

History records that Frederick Charrington became one of the most well-known temperance activists in England. He renounced his share of the family fortune and devoted the rest of his life to the ministry of freeing men and women from the curse of alcoholism.

Here was a man who, when confronted with the wrong, turned away from it and pursued the right steadfastly in spite of great personal cost.

What about you and I? When we are confronted with our sin are we so grieved that we mourn and tear our clothes? Are we also willing to follow the Lord in holiness of life?

There's a treasure much greater than any to be found in a bucket of dirt from the gold city gem mine, it's the treasure of intimacy with our Lord. But the treasure is only found by those who are working to do what they know is right and who are willing to do what the Lord asks.

-Chapter Eight-

A New Beginning

It was a bright Sunday morning in 18th century London, but Robert Robinson's mood was anything but sunny. All along the street there were people hurrying to church, but in the midst of the crowd Robinson was a lonely man. The sound of church bells reminded him of years past when his faith in God was strong and the church was an integral part of his life. It had been years since he set foot in a church—years of wandering, disillusionment, and gradual defection from the God he once loved. That love for God—once fiery and passionate—had slowly burned out within him, leaving him dark and cold inside. Robinson heard the clip-clop, clip-clop of a horse-drawn cab approaching behind him. Turning, he lifted his hand to hail the driver. But then he saw that the cab was occupied by a young woman dressed in finery for the Lord's Day. He waved the driver on, but the woman in the carriage ordered the carriage to be stopped.

"Sir, I'd be happy to share this carriage with you," she said to Robinson. "Are you going to church?" Robinson was about to decline, then he paused. "Yes," he said at last. "I am going to church." He stepped into the carriage and sat down beside the young woman. As the carriage rolled forward Robert Robinson and the woman exchanged introductions. There was a flash of recognition in her eyes when he stated his name. "That's an interesting coincidence," she said, reaching into her purse. She withdrew a small book of inspirational verse, opened it to a ribbon-bookmark, and handed the book to him. "I was just reading a verse by a poet named Robert Robinson. Could it be…?"

He took the book, nodding. "Yes, I wrote these words years ago." "Oh, how wonderful!" she exclaimed. "Imagine! I'm sharing a carriage with the author of these very lines!"

But Robinson barely heard her. He was absorbed in the words he was reading. They were words that would one day be set to music and become a great hymn of the faith, familiar to generations of Christians:

Come, Thou Fount of every blessing,

Tune my heart to sing Thy grace'

Streams of mercy, never ceasing,

Call for songs of loudest praise.

His eyes slipped to the bottom of the page where he read:

Prone to wander, Lord, I feel it —

Prone to leave the God I love;

Here's my heart, O take and seal it,

Seal it for Thy courts above.

He could barely read the last few lines through the tears that brimmed in his eyes. "I wrote these words — and I've lived these words. 'Prone to wander…prone to leave the God I love.'"

The woman suddenly understood. "You also wrote, 'Here's my heart, O take and seal it.' You can offer your heart again to God, Mr. Robinson. It's not too late."

And it wasn't too late for Robert Robinson. In that moment he turned his heart back to God and walked with him the rest of his days. [Ron Lee Davis, Courage to Begin Again, (Harvest House, Eugene, OR; 1978), pp. 145-147]

Where are you at in your walk with the Lord today? Like the hymn writer have you found yourself drifting away from the Lord's arms of love? Has the fire that once burned with passion for Christ grown cold?

God's message for you is that new beginnings are possible. Just like in the time of Josiah, King of Judah, just like in 18th century England God longs to draw wayward children back home, God longs to stoke the flames of our hearts with revival.

As we draw near to the end on I'd like us to look together at the last of the revivals that swept the nation of Judah and ask ourselves one last time, Why then? What did these people do that led to renewed fellowship with God? The answers I believe are key to us if we wish to experience revival in the present tense.

The first answer is that they

1. Renewed their Promise

"The king stood by the pillar and renewed the covenant in the presence of the LORD — to follow the LORD and keep his commands, regulations and decrees with all his heart and all his soul, thus confirming the words of the covenant written in this book. Then all the people pledged themselves to the covenant." (2 Kings 23:3 NIV)

First of all they took a stand. They said look we've been going in the wrong direction, but right here, right now, we're going back on the right track. We're renewing our covenant with the Lord. We will follow, we will serve.

What about you? Has God been tugging at your heart? Has this book been God's wake-up call to you. Are you ready to come home like the Prodigal son? It all begins with a new beginning, a renewal of your covenant. That doesn't mean you're being re-saved, Josiah and the people weren't saying "we haven't been your people but now we want to be again." No they were saying "we haven't lived up to our end of the bargain, but from this point forward, with your help we're going to act like the people of God. We want to come home"

They renewed their Promise. Next they...

2. Remembered God's Providence

"The king gave this order to all the people: "Celebrate the Passover to the LORD your God, as it is written in this Book of the Covenant." (2 Kings: 23:21 NKJV)

Note that this is the first time Passover was correctly celebrated since before the time of David. The Passover was all about remembering God's help in ages past. It was all about recalling God's saving deeds for His people. The significance of this act is the role it has in helping to renew the faith of the people--

the God who worked miraculously on our behalf in the past is a God worthy to be trusted now.

We have a need for the same type of remembrance. First of all of the work of Christ to pay for our sins, but also to remember God's saving work in a personal way. We need to remember how God brought us to faith, and the things that He's done in our lives. We have a need to recount that story to others as a ritual of remembrance.

The next thing I notice that Josiah and the people did which was a crucial part of revival is that they...

3. Reformed their Practices

"Furthermore, Josiah got rid of the mediums and spiritists, the household gods, the idols and all the other detestable things seen in Judah and Jerusalem. This he did to fulfill the requirements of the law written in the book that Hilkiah the priest had discovered in the temple of the LORD." (2 Kings 23:24 NKJV)

This is of course the repentance theme which we have seen in every one of these chapters on not because I've chosen to emphasize it, but because it is always a part of the story when revival comes. Without repentance there is no revival or perhaps it's the other way around.

The danger of course is that we might be tempted to believe that God's blessings, even our salvation are dependent upon our behavior, or somehow a reward for right living.

In response to that kind of thinking Oswald Chambers wrote... "It is not repentance that saves me; repentance is the sign that I realize what God has done in Christ Jesus... Is it my obedience that puts me right with God? Never! I am put right with God because prior to all else, Christ died... By the miracle of God's grace I stand justified, not because of anything I have done, but because of what Jesus has done... Sinful men and women can be changed into new creatures by the marvelous work of God in Christ Jesus."

That change is evidenced in repentance; a key ingredient of any true revival. The final thing I note that is clearly a part of revival is that they...

4. Rekindled their Passion

"Neither before nor after Josiah was there a king like him who turned to the LORD as he did — with all his heart and with all his soul and with all his strength, in accordance with all the Law of Moses." (2 Kings 23:25 NIV)

Josiah, the Scripture is careful to note, was passionate in his devotion to the Lord.

In 1746 Jonathan Edwards published a book, The Religious Affections, in which he argued that "true religion must consist very much in the affections," Edwards believed that one of the chief works of Satan was to convince men that emotions have no place in spiritual life, that emotional responses are to be guarded against. This mindset, he warned, will "bring all religion to a mere lifeless formality, and effectually shut out the power of godliness" Edwards went on to say, "There is no true religion where there is no religious affection....If the great things of religion are rightly understood, they will affect the heart ."

One of the undeniable features of revival is that God's people get passionate about serving God, with all of their heart, soul and strength. When we understand what Christ has done for us, we can't help but be filled with inexpressible joy.

Revival is by necessity a heart centered activity, love is the motive of repentance.

As Robert Robinson wrote and lived out we are very much prone to wander, prone to leave the God we love. But as he did we can find the road back, we can experience a new beginning when we say: Here's my heart, O take and seal it, Seal it for Thy courts above.

-Chapter Nine-

Making Room for the Move

This final chapter is one that I had not planned on including originally, but I think it is apropos for this journey. We have spoken a lot of repentance, revival but I think to seal the work we must speak of how to make room for God.

In 2 Kings 4:8-10 (NKJV) we find the following story,

"Now there came a day when Elisha passed over to Shunem, where there was a prominent woman, and she persuaded him to eat food. And so it was, as often as he passed by, he turned in there to eat food. She said to her husband, "Behold now, I perceive that this is a holy man of God passing by us continually. Please, let us make a little walled upper chamber and let us set a bed for him there, and a table and a chair and a lampstand; and it shall be, when he comes to us, that he can turn in there.""

I have always been intrigued by this passage. Here is this prominent woman who is able to persuade Elisha to stop in for food. But not only does she do that, she recognizes the importance of having the prophet in her home. From this story we recognize several keys in making room for the Holy Spirit. The first being...

There is no Room in the Present Structure

She says to her husband, let's build a room on top of our house. There was no room to house the prophet and so she recognized the need to expand their structure. How often do check our structure to make sure there is room for God to reside? Do we have room for God to move?

In the same chapter Elisha meets the widow woman and instructs her in the miracle of the oil. We are asking, praying, seeking but it seems we have no room. We will always get the level of revival that we make room for.

Just as the woman ran out of jars, the oil quits flowing when capacity of expansion has been filled.

The second thing we realize is...

You cannot raise the roof without a firm foundation

This couple was able to build upon what they already have. Many of us don't have a habitation with God because we don't have a foundation capable of handling the weight of habitation. 1 Cor. 3:11 states, "For no man can lay a foundation other than the one which is laid, which is Jesus Christ."

The church cries out "Show me your glory" but they don't realize that His glory is the full weight of his authority. Some of us get a visitation but then we go back to normal life because we don't have foundation to build upon to sustain a habitation. He pours in the new wine and we experience spontaneous combustion because we have old wineskins. We haven't prepared or made room for the move of God.

I think of the parable of the man who built his house upon the sand. What happened? The rains came and the winds blew and his house was destroyed. Without a firm foundation, the waves of temptation will come and the winds of doctrine will blow and you'll find yourself bankrupt and without His presence.

The third key is…

**It's not just enough to raise the roof,
but you must also furnish the room.**

They didn't just make a room, they created an environment conducive for habitation.

A Bed

The first article they put in the room was a bed. The bed represents the place of rest. Psalm 37:7 says, "Quiet down before God, be prayerful before him. Don't bother with those who climb the ladder, who elbow their way to the top." (MSG)

We will rest on our laurels, our abilities and our gifts but there will be now habitation until we learn to rest in Him. You cannot elbow your way into His presence, it's just not possible. We have to learn to abide, to wait. I remember as a boy we had "tarrying meetings" where we would just wait on the Lord. And boy oh boy did He show up – but that's just it. Even then, it was just a visitation.

A Table

The second article they placed in the room was a table. It represents the place of communion, a place to be fed, a place of fellowship. We want habitation, but not the time it takes.

Zacchaeus climbs into the tree to see Jesus – to see his power and his works. Jesus wanted to commune with him and calls him out of the tree of spectating to come to his house.

There can be no habitation if there is no time of communion. You can't just eat and run. He wants you to come and dine, to spend some time.

A Chair

The third article that was placed in the room was that of a chair. This a place of total support – total dependence. When I sit in a chair, I am expecting it to hold me up. We must have total reliance on Him to hold us.

We have to learn to actually live out Proverbs 3:5 "Trust in the Lord and lean not on your own understanding." We quote it, but do we live it?

Habitation comes when we don't rely on our reputation, contacts, education, intelligence, or even relationships to hold us up.

Micah 3:11 says, "Her leaders judge for a bribe, her priests teach for a price and her prophets tell fortunes for money. Yet they look for the Lord's support and say, "Is not the Lord among us? No disaster will come upon us."

We can't do our own thing and expect God to show up. Find out what god is doing and show up.

A Lamp

The fourth article was the Lamp. This represents the WORD of God – illumination. You cannot have permanent habitation without the Light of the Word.

You have to dig it out for yourself – this is where revival comes from. Without knowing the Word, you cannot know Him.

How long does an ember last if the fire is gone? Jeremiah said, "The WORD is like fire in my bones."

David said the WORD was his protection from sin: "I have hid thy word in my heart that I might not sin against thee." (Ps. 119:11)

The WORD brings direction to our lives, "Thy word is a lamp unto my feet and light unto my path." (Ps. 119:5)

Revival cannot and will not be permanent without the light of His WORD.

The reason many of us never experience revival or a habitation is because we haven't furnished the room so there can be a move in.

I want to end this book with a few questions:

1. Do you have room? Have you boxed God out? Has the oil quit flowing?
2. Have you established a firm foundation? Can you handle the weightiness? Can you support the fresh move?
3. Have you furnished your life with rest, communion, dependency? Do you have provision for light? Do you need fire?

God promises to revive His people. **He wants revival more than you do!** Wait in earnest expectation –there's a fresh move about to take place.

WILL YOU NOT REVIVE US *AND*
BRING US TO LIFE AGAIN,
THAT YOUR PEOPLE MAY REJOICE IN YOU?
PSALM 85:6

A Prophetic Word about Revival

"The Fountains of the Deep are about to rise again"

"…on that day all the springs of the great deep burst forth, and the floodgates of the heavens were opened."   Genesis 7:22 (NIV)

I heard the Lord say, "The Fountains of the deep are about to rise again, but this time they are bringing my mercy. For I am bringing them forth not in judgment or in wrath, but this time they will come forth in great mercy to bring a cleansing power to the nations through my church."

I was woken from a dead sleep with this word. I got out of my hotel bed in Oklahoma City to write it down. I stood at the window of my room after writing this down and was taken into what I can only describe as an open vision. Before my eyes across the state I saw huge gushers coming up out of the ground and I knew that this was going to happen across the nation. I was then taken into living rooms in major cities. I was standing and observing as

89

people across the nation gathered in their homes to pray.

As they began to pray, I watched as whirlpools would form in the midst of their group. These pools began to swirl, increasing in speed as the fervency of their prayer increased. As their fervency increased the water would begin to trickle out of the whirlpool. Some were content with the trickling. But there were others who were not satisfied. They contended all the more.

As time went on, certain whirlpools became fountains. Some shot up only a foot, others 3, 4, 5 or even 10 feet. Fervency increased. The Fountains increased. Over time as unity and fervency increased these fountains shot through the roof and began to rain over the cities. I saw as floods began to form, not causing destruction. No, they weren't floods of destruction, these were floods of cleansing. These floods weren't from the depths of the earth, they were from the depths of the Heart of God. They began to flow through the cities, connecting to other fountains, until I saw the nation being flooded.

I said, "Lord, what does this mean?" He said, "This is what I desire to do. If my people will lay aside their agendas and opinions and simply seek my face with fervency, I will pour out a cleansing from the depths of my heart. I will cause the fountains of the deep to be released once again. This will not only touch America, but this will flow throughout the nations of the Earth. As my people unite across their borders and cities and nations, I will bring a cleansing like never before."

I was instantly back in my hotel room. As I stood there looking back out over Oklahoma City, a sprinkler head broke and water began to gush into the parking lot. I took this as a confirmation of what the Lord showed me. Get ready, He is releasing the Fountains of the Deep. Cleansing is coming from the Heart of the Father – Mercy will flood our streets in this hour.

Meet the Author

Jacob Biswell is a prophet, revivalist, and father with signs and wonders following his ministry. Dynamic shifts and powerful unlockings are commonplace around him.

As a prophetic voice, he is a highly sought-after speaker, both nationally and internationally. He speaks at conferences, churches, and other events, activating and empowering people to enter their destiny, grab hold of their dreams, and receive their healing.

Jacob is apostolically aligned with TRIBE Network under Apostle Ryan LeStrange. He serves as a Zone Leader for Tribe. In addition, he has an accountability board consisting of Apostle Brent Douglas of New Zealand, Prophet Birdella Tucker of California, and Dr. Candi MacAlpine of California.

He leads a local Revival Hub in Texas called the Equipping Center, where his focus is raise up healthy prophets and a prophetic culture.

Jacob is married to Anna Katheryn, is a daddy to two children, and resides in Texas.

Other Resources by Jacob Biswell

www.jacobbiswell.com

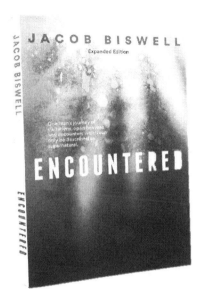

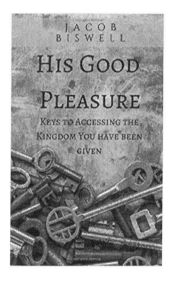

Made in the USA
Columbia, SC
11 October 2018